HOMEWORK HELP
ON THE
INTERNET

Marianne J. Dyson

SCHOLASTIC REFERENCE

This book is dedicated to the children of cyberspace, including Thomas and Scott; to all the wonderful volunteer Web masters; to the world's best husband (mine!); and to two extraordinary editors, Elysa Jacobs and Mary Jones.

Library of Congress Cataloging-in-Publication Data available.

ISBN 0-439-20892-0

10 9 8 7 6 5 4 3 2 1   0/0 01 02 03 04

⁺he U.S.A.   23
g, August 2000

CONTENTS

1: INTRODUCTION

◀WELCOME TO CYBERSPACE

Got homework? Need help? Welcome to cyberspace—the ultimate information source. Want a photo of bacteria? Practice with math facts? Quotes for a history debate? It's all out there in cyberspace.

Just because the information is out there doesn't mean it is easy to find. Using a search engine or a "Homework Help" site does not always produce useful results. There might not be any sites listed on your topic, or there could be so many it would take days to check them all.

This book is designed to take you directly to the information you need. All sites listed were carefully reviewed. They had to be safe (no violent, hateful, or sexual content), and they had to be *useful*. Each site was tested with actual homework assignments from elementary and middle-school textbooks. Sites selected used reliable sources and had addresses unlikely to change.

To use this book, first read the Safe Surfing sections. Then, go to the index to see if the topic you need is listed with a page number. If it is not, flip to the subject section that relates to your homework assignment. Check the general sources for that subject. If you still need help, use the recommended search engines and general homework help sites in Chapter 8.

During your trips to cyberspace, don't be surprised if you get distracted. It is easy for hours to zip past while you read about exciting people and places or try that skill game one more time. Like too much dessert, your brain may even fill up with so many facts at once that you suffer "information overload."

To avoid these problems write down homework questions and key words before going online. Set a time limit for the session. If you can't find information on a question or topic right away, skip it. When you find lots of sites, check facts from three sources and move on. Go back for more detail only if you have time. Once your questions are answered, sign off and get your homework done!

Information from cyberspace is useful for more than homework.

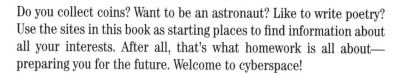

Do you collect coins? Want to be an astronaut? Like to write poetry? Use the sites in this book as starting places to find information about all your interests. After all, that's what homework is all about—preparing you for the future. Welcome to cyberspace!

SAFE SURFING
Permission
When someone says you can use a computer to access the Internet, assume that that is all you have permission to do. If you want to do anything in addition to clicking on links and looking at the data that comes up, be sure to ask!

Unless you have permission to do so, don't:

- Download large files that can tie up a computer for a long time
- Register for free software, free e-mail accounts, free Web pages, or free chat services
- Print very long documents, especially if you have a color printer

User Names and Passwords
Before you start, make sure that you have all of your user names and passwords handy. Try to choose passwords that are 10 or more characters long and include numbers and symbols. This will make it harder to guess. It is okay to write this password down. Just don't share it while online or via e-mail.

Only send e-mail from your own account. Don't assume that it is okay to write and send e-mail using someone else's account. If you do, you are pretending to be someone you aren't.

Keeping Secrets Secret
Unfortunately, there are criminals who surf the Internet looking for victims. You don't have to be one of them! Follow these rules to keep your secrets safe.

1. Never give out your last name, parents' first names, address, phone number, credit card number or expiration date, or school name. People can use this information to cause you harm.

2. Do not send regular mail (snail mail) to people you meet online without your parents' permission. They can use the return address or postmark on the envelope to tell where you live.

3. Do not send your passwords or other personal information (see item 1) to anyone via e-mail or in a chat—even if they are someone you know.

4. Watch out for tricks. If someone sends you a message saying they are from your online service and need your password, they are lying. Your online service will not lose your password. If you lose it, they will ask you to choose a new one.

5. Don't give out the last names of your friends, teachers, or neighbors without their permission. Clever con artists can use this data to go after them. They can also use it to figure out who you are and where you live.

Reporting Unsightly Sites

If you come across a site that scares or sickens you, quickly hit "Back" on your Web browser. Write down the address (the URL) of the page you were on just before you got to the offensive site. Give this to a parent or teacher. They can then report the link as well as the offensive site to the appropriate Web master.

Protecting Yourself from Viruses

Computer viruses, like human viruses, can be a nuisance, or they can be deadly serious. There are two ways to get infected: through a disk or through a network connection to another computer. Here are a few things you can do to protect your computer and the data stored on it:

1. Make sure your computer has current anti-virus software loaded. Old software will not protect you from new viruses.

2. Do not forward warnings about viruses. E-mail messages warning about viruses are almost always hoaxes, and often are used to spread the virus. If you receive such a message, do not open any attachments it may have.

3. Do not forward chain letters. These letters are often tricks used by scam artists to collect e-mail addresses.

Saving Data (Downloading)

There are four ways to save data from the Internet.

1. Scan and take notes.

2. Print out pages.

3. Copy and paste parts of pages into files.

4. Download the page or image.

1. Scanning/Navigating Tips

Most online pages are too big to fit on a computer screen. To view other parts of the page, use your cursor to slide the square on the right side of the window up and down, or use the little up and down arrows.

When you select a link that brings up a new page, you can always return to the previous page using the "Back" (or arrow) on your browser. If you change your mind while a page is loading, select the red "Stop" sign option on your browser. (It may have an X on it.)

Some sites listed in this book contain ads. Ads are usually at the top of the page. Some flash at you, while others have text questions scrolling across. If you click on one by mistake, use the "Back" option to return to the page you want.

Beware of ads that pop up with an X in a red dot and a warning that your computer does not have the best connection or program. If you click on the X in the corner, instead of closing, these ads pop to full size. You can't move these windows out of the way. If you click on one of these by mistake, use the "Back" or "Stop" option.

When taking notes, be sure to write down the URL address and date. You may need to include this information in a bibliography.

2. Printing Tips

Some Web sites have dozens of pages. Before you print, set the Print/File option to "pages 1 to 2" instead of "all," unless you really want all the pages. If you don't, you could end up with lots of useless pages spewing from your printer.

Some online pages have more than one frame, such as a banner that stays at the top of the page even when you scroll down. Be sure to make sure you have clicked on the correct frame when you print.

Otherwise, you may end up printing out ads rather than information for your homework.

3. Copying and Pasting Tips

If you need only a paragraph out of a long article, don't waste time and disk space downloading the whole thing. Highlight and then copy the text. Next, open a new document in your word processor. (A blank e-mail works also.) Paste the text into the document. If the text contains hot links, be warned that clicking on them—even after you get off the Internet—may activate your browser.

Be sure to record the URL, date, and any copyright information for your bibliography.

4. Downloading Tips

For images such as maps, place your cursor over the image and click the right mouse button (or simply keep the mouse button held down on Macs). This will bring up a window where you will select "Save As" to save the image to your computer's hard drive. Unless you are planning to enlarge an image, you don't need a high resolution version.

If you want to store the page just as it looks online for studying off-line later, use the File "Save As" option and choose an .htm file type. To view it later, bring up your browser and open the file. You do not have to be online.

Many Web sites include sounds, animations, calculations, and other advanced features. When displaying these pages, your browser will check to see if the programs needed are already installed on your computer. If so, the ads will flash and sounds will play without you doing anything. If these programs are not on your computer, some of the page's features may not work. A window will pop up asking if you want to download the software. Do not say yes unless you have the appropriate permission to do so.

SEARCHING THE WEB

Hot Links and Dead Ends: Using Search Engines

Search engines are programs that check the World Wide Web for pages that contain the word or phrase you ask it to find. A search brings up a list of titles and links. (Links are generally underlined or in a different color than the other text.) Click on the link to be taken to a new Web page. To return to the list of links after viewing a new page, simply click on the "Back" option on your browser.

If a link brings up an error message, do not be alarmed—nothing is wrong with your computer. Usually it means that the address is no good, or the computer called is not working. Simply click "Back" on your Web browser and try another link.

The list of links you get from conducting a search will not include all sites on the World Wide Web. Search engines flip through a database of pages. Each search engine has its own database. This database is like a phone book. Some of these have Web pages and some do not. Others will be listed by their names and not by their subjects. Still others may not be included in that particular search engine. This is especially true of engines designed for kids. Having a smaller "phone book" to look through cuts down on the time you spend checking out links.

Search engines are computer programs. They do only what they are told. If you spell a search word wrong, they will search on it anyway. (Word processors and Internet browsers can check your spelling for you!) Computers also do not know that when you search on "rock" (as in volcanic), you are not looking for rock 'n' roll bands. Therefore you will get a lot of sites that are not what you want.

Before you do a search, check out the list of Web sites provided under the subject headings in this book. These sites have been checked for you and judged to be useful for helping with homework. Bookmark them or add them to your "Favorites" list in your browser so you can jump right to them when you need help.

LIMITING YOUR SEARCH

Let's assume you have to do a report on an American president, but you want more data before picking one about which to write. You go to Yahoo (http://www.yahoo.com) and type in the words "American president." You press Enter on your keyboard or click on the Search button to begin the search.

The result is a list of thousands of Web pages! Many of these are totally useless, such as advertisements for resorts and movies that have the words "American" and "president" in them. You decide to use Yahoo's kids' search engine, Yahooligans.

Once again, you enter the words "American president." You get more than 200 Web pages. This is better, but not much! The resorts and movie sites are gone, but there are still some useless ones such as one about the president of the American Red Cross.

To avoid those kinds of sites, you can tell the search engine to search only for sites that have the words "American" and "president" next to each other in that order. You do this by putting quotation marks around the words.

You enter "American president" with quotation marks into Yahooligans and press Enter. You get only three Web sites. One site is a repeat. However, these two sites have the exact information you need: a picture and short biography of each president. You can now choose a president for your report. Then you can return to the search engine and enter the first and last name in quotes to find more about that particular president.

Safe Search Engines

CyberSleuth Kids—This search engine has thousands of safe sites in its database. **http://cybersleuth-kids.com**

CyberSitter—**http://www.solidoak.com**

KidsClick—Choose a subject area to narrow your search, then either use the topics or search on a keyword. You can choose whether or not you want to view photos. **http://sunsite.berkeley.edu/KidsClick!/**

KidsNook—This kid-friendly site has helpful categories to make finding information easier. The site is expanding its database every day so check back often. **http://www.kidsnook.com**

Yahooligans—This is probably the most comprehensive of all the kids' search engines. If you are having trouble locating information on a specific topic, check out Yahooligans. **http://www.yahooligans.com**

"NETIQUETTE"

In every society, there are rules for proper behavior. In cyberspace, where no one can hear your tone of voice or see you wink, these rules are especially important. No rule can stop some people from being jerks. Nor can it stop someone from being so sensitive they get their feelings hurt by every little remark. But by following the rules, you can help avoid and limit the damage caused either by accident or by a few troublemakers.

1. Do not use foul language. Besides being a rude thing to do, some online services routinely scan e-mail, chats, and bulletin boards for bad words. If they find offensive material, they will terminate your account (and that of your parents!). They do not give you a chance to explain or apologize.

2. DO NOT TYPE IN ALL CAPITAL LETTERS! This is considered shouting. It is okay to capitalize one word to make a POINT.

3. Do not hold down one key. It is obnoxious!!!!!!!!!!!!!!!!!!!! and considered very childish.

4. Do not "spam." Spamming is sending a message to lots of e-mail addresses (usually people not known to the sender) without permission. If you receive a spam, such as an ad from a stranger for their Web site, do not reply to it because they may put you on a permanent mailing list.

5. Do not post someone else's words, pictures, artwork, or animation without their permission. You should also not pretend to be some other real person such as a celebrity.

6. Lurk before you speak. Before posting a message to a bulletin board, read messages already there. This will keep you from asking questions that have already been answered. Likewise, when joining a chat, listen to what others are talking about before jumping in with your own message.

7. Do not forward e-mails without the permission of the sender. They may not appreciate your giving out their e-mail address. Most people forget to ask, so if you don't want a message of yours to be forwarded, clearly say that it is private at the top and/or bottom of the message.

8. Keep your sense of humor. The use of "emoticons" such as :) (for "smiley face") and <g> (for "grin") avoids people taking your comments the wrong way.

9. Learn and follow the rules of your online service, bulletin boards, and chat rooms. Check carefully if it is okay before posting any items for sale or doing any surveys. For chats, always read the FAQ (Frequently Asked Questions) file.

For more information on Netiquette, check these sites:

A helpful Netiquette guide:
http://www.albion.com/netiquette/corerules.html

This site covers not only Netiquette, but also the basics of surfing the Net.

http://www.learnthenet.com/english/section/intbas.html

BIBLIOGRAPHIES AND REFERENCES

Web stories, photos, animations, logos, and even messages on public bulletin boards are all protected by copyright laws. Posting information in any of those formats on the Internet is considered publication under U.S. laws. Only the creator of the work can grant the right to copy, or copyright, it. You are allowed (under what are called Fair Use laws) to copy items to your personal computer and print them out for use in a debate or school report—as long as you give proper credit to the source. You are not allowed to make copies for your friends, post it on a Web page, or otherwise publish someone else's work without their permission.

Material provided by a branch or agency of the U.S. government—unless stated otherwise—is not copyrighted. The public (taxpayers) paid for these things to be produced, so they belong to the public. This means that you do not have to get permission to use text or images produced by the military or government agencies. URLs including a .gov or .mil indicate if a site is run by the government. There is one restriction on the use of government materials, though: They cannot be used to sell a product. For example, a company can't use a government photo of a cow to advertise ice cream. Therefore, if your homework project involves creating a poster to sell a product, you should avoid using government images. Government agencies sometimes do use copyright materials, especially photos and quotes, on their sites. You do not have to get permission to use them, but you do have to give credit to the artist or author.

Giving credit so that a reader can find the source you used is what bibliographies are all about.

What Information Do You Need for a Bibliography?

1. The first thing you need is the address, or URL, of the site. The URL is almost always (some advertisers cover it up) listed in the address window of your browser. You can simply copy it down. If you have access to a printer, you can get an even better record by printing at least one page. The URL is automatically printed in the lower left-hand corner.

2. Another thing you need for a bibliography is the date of access. This is important because Web pages change all the time. You can simply write down the date you visited the site, or print out a page from the site.

3. Another date you need is the date the article was written or the image was created. Look near the title or at the bottom of the page. If the article does not have a date on it, use the "date last updated" at the bottom of the page. If there is no date, make a note.

4. Copy down the title of the article or image. If it has no title, use the sponsor (company, agency, or organization) name that is hosting the site. If there is no title or sponsor name, use the first sentence or file name.

5. Find and record the names of the authors, artists, or contributors associated with the article or image. The first place to look is under the title or image. If there is no byline or credit line, look for icons that say "About Us" or "Contact Us" or an address at the bottom of the page. You may have to go to the home page for the site to find this. If no specific author or artist is listed, but there is a

sponsor for the site, then use that name under "author" in the bibliography.

6. Finally, if there is more than one article or image on the page, describe which one you used. The description can be a single word, a sentence, or a file name that you clicked on or downloaded.

There are several different styles—all correct—to use in a bibliography. It is important to be consistent and include all the key information. Ask yourself if your teacher could find your source using the information you provided. Here is one suggested format:

Author. Title (of the article or image or page). Date of Publication. Date of Access. [online] <URL in the form **http://address/filename**>. Optional (use especially if there is more than one image or article on the page): Description of the article or image (the file name, image number, or .jpg file name).

Example:

U.S. Fish and Wildlife Service Photo by Kent Olson. Photograph taken near the Red Rock Lakes National Wildlife Refuge in Montana. No date given. Accessed 2-09-00. [online] <**http://endangered.fws.gov/uppermo.html**> Photo of a mountain and valley in the Yellowstone ecosystem. Image file r6esyslc.jpg.

Use More Than One Reference

When doing research for a report, it is important to use more than one reference. This is especially true when using Internet sources. Most Web sites are not professionally edited. Therefore, they often contain poor grammar, typos, and incomplete or incorrect information. Even the most reliable sites—ones run by government and academic groups—have their share of incorrect dates and misspelled names. By checking facts from several Web sites and offline resources, you will get correct and more complete information. To help you tell which sites to trust and different ways to list references, check out the Web pages below.

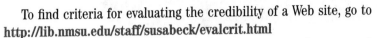

To find criteria for evaluating the credibility of a Web site, go to
http://lib.nmsu.edu/staff/susabeck/evalcrit.html
You can find different ways to site online references at
http://tekmom.com/cite/index.html
and
http://www.lafayette.edu/library/guides/cite.html

HOW TO USE ADDRESSES

One Web site can contain hundreds of individual addresses, like an
apartment building contains hundreds of individual units and those
units in turn have many rooms. Having specific page addresses saves
you from visiting all the pages and rooms to find the ones that can
help with homework. Be sure to enter the URLs exactly as shown. If
you want to go to the "apartment building" or home page of a site,
chop off everything in the address after the first /. For example,
http://forum.swarthmore.edu/dr.math/drmath.elem.html/
mathgrepform.html
would become simply
http://forum.swarthmore.edu.
If a page isn't "found," check that the URL is entered properly. If it
still doesn't load, try chopping off pieces of the address, one / section
at a time.

2: AMERICAN HISTORY

◀GENERAL AMERICAN HISTORY SOURCES

To find basic information about each of the 50 states, go to
http://www.50states.com/fileindx.htm

To find a list of national historic sites organized by subject, go to this site. Don't hesitate to explore the links to find more in-depth information about specific topics.
http://www.cr.nps.gov/catsig.htm

Use this site to search for names, topics, or dates relating to major historical events.
http://www.historychannel.com

Use this site to find transcripts and photos of the original documents of American history. Part I contains some modern documents. Part II has a chronological index. Don't miss the "Exhibits Hall" listing special features. Use the search link to check archives for images of events or people. Exhibits Hall Main Page:
http://www.nara.gov/exhall/exhibits.html

American Originals Part I:
http://www.nara.gov/exhall/originals/original.html

American Originals Part II:
http://www.nara.gov/exhall/originals/origina2.html

To find biographies and photographs of important Americans, go to
http://www.npg.si.edu/exh/brady/gallery/bradindx.html

Check out this wide array of links to specific topics within American history.
http://www.rr.gmcs.k12.nm.us/domagala.history.htm

Use this chronological list to locate primary source documents, such as the U.S. Constitution, Mayflower Compact, Gettysburg Address, and treaties with Native Americans and foreign countries.
http://www.yale.edu/lawweb/avalon/chrono.htm

North America Before 1775
To see photos and illustrations of Plymouth Colony, go to
http://etext.virginia.edu/users/deetz/Plymouth/addisonimg.html

To read about the founding of Plymouth, the Pilgrims, and the *Mayflower,* go to
http://pilgrims.net/plymouth/history/

To read biographies of Columbus, Erikson, Cook, Magellan, Cortes, and other explorers, go to
http://www.bham.wednet.edu/land.htm

To access a time line that describes each significant date in American history, go to
http://www.historyplace.com/unitedstates/revolution/rev-early.htm

To read biographies about early world explorers such as Cook, Magellan, Drake, Cabot, and Hudson, head to
http://www.mariner.org/age/menu.html

Who were the pilgrims? Who were the Wampanoag? Did they eat popcorn at Thanksgiving? To answer these questions about early Americans, go to
http://www.plimoth.org/Library/library.htm

For information about and maps of the original 13 colonies, go to
http://www.seanet.com/users/pamur/13colony.html

The American Revolution (1775–1783)
To see newspapers, maps, magazines, and writings from early America, check out this site.
http://earlyamerica.com/earlyamerica/index.html

Need to know about the American Revolution? About the people and places that played decisive roles in the war? This is the site for you. It contains detailed time lines and biographical information about both American and British leaders.

http://www.dell.homestead.com/revwar/files/index.htm

To view a photo gallery of George Washington, go to

http://www.historyplace.com/unitedstates/revolution/wash-pix/gallery.htm

To read the text of the Declaration of Independence and find biographical information about its signers, head to

http://www.law.indiana.edu/uslawdocs/declaration.html

To read about the American Revolution and the background of the signers of the Declaration of Independence, check out

http://www.worldquest.com/law/declare.htm

A New Nation (1783–1800)

For an explanation of the U.S. Constitution and its Amendments, go to

http://gi.grolier.com/presidents/nbk/side/conttext.html

To read about the major battles and the role of women during the War of 1812, go to

http://members.tripod.com/~war1812/

To read about Shays' Rebellion, go to

http://www.calliope.org/shays/shays2.html

For information about the Northwest Ordinance, go to

http://www.earlyamerica.com/earlyamerica/milestones/index.html

To read about the War of 1812 from the Native American perspective, go to

http://www-personal.umich.edu/~ksands/War.html

To read the text of the Articles of Confederation and link to Thomas Jefferson's autobiography, go to
http://www.yale.edu/lawweb/avalon/artconf.htm

Westward Expansion (1800–1900)
To read about the history of railroads in the United States, go to
http://www.blm.gov/education/railroads/trans.html

For information about the Louisiana Purchase, go to
http://www.earlyamerica.com/earlyamerica/milestones/index.html

To read the Homestead Act of 1862, go to
http://www.geocities.com/Heartland/Bluffs/3010/homestd.htm

To read eyewitness accounts of the Battle at Wounded Knee, Custer's Last Stand, and a train robbery, go to
http://www.ibiscom.com/owfrm.htm

To read about the Oregon Trail, go to
http://www.isu.edu/~trinmich/Allabout.html

To read about the Mexican War (1846–1848), go to
http://www.lnstar.com/mall/texasinfo/mexicow.htm

To learn about the Lewis and Clark expedition, go to
http://www.pbs.org/lewisandclark/

To read biographies of people influential in the American West, go to
http://www.pbs.org/weta/thewest/wpages/wpgs400/w400_001.htm

For information about slavery in the American West, Native American removal including the Trail of Tears, the Dred Scott decision, and Lincoln's "A House Divided" speech, go to
http://www.pbs.org/wgbh/aia/part4/4narr4.html

To read about the Transcontinental Railroad, go to
http://www.sfmuseum.org/hist1/rail.html

To read accounts of pioneer women who were part of the California Gold Rush, go to

http://www.sfmuseum.org/hist5/foremoms.html

What was so important about the Alamo? Read all about the place where Davy Crockett, James Bowie, and William Travis fought and died for Texas independence from Mexico at

http://www.thealamo.org/index.html

To read about early roads, canals, rivers, and railroads in the United States and see illustrations with drawings, go to

http://xroads.virginia.edu/~MA98/haven/transport/front.html

A Nation Divided (1820–1865)

For information about Abraham Lincoln, check out this site that includes a time line that features photos, links to speeches, documents, and Lincoln's autobiography.

http://www.historyplace.com/lincoln/index.html

To read an eyewitness account of Andrew Johnson's impeachment, the story of Frederick Douglass's escape from slavery, and a description of a slave ship, go to

http://www.ibiscom.com/19frm.htm

For information about the Emancipation Proclamation, go to

http://www.nara.gov/exhall/featured-document/eman/emanproc.html

To read about the Lincoln-Douglas Debates of 1858, go to

http://www.outfitters.com/illinois/history/civil/debates.html

For information about the Underground Railroad, go to

http://www.worldbook.com/fun/aajourny/html/bh040.html

Read about the Missouri Compromise at this site. Click on "Struggle to Abolish Slavery" to read biographies of Sojourner Truth, Harriet Tubman, and Frederick Douglass.

http://www.worldbook.com/fun/aajourny/html/bh041.html

The Civil War (1861–1865)

For comprehensive information about the people and places of the American Civil War, go to
http://americancivilwar.com/

To see a time line and photographs of the Civil War, go to
http://www.historyplace.com/civilwar/index.html

Read eyewitness accounts of the Battle of Antietam, the surrender at Appomattox, the death of John Wilkes Booth, and the death of Abraham Lincoln at
http://www.ibiscom.com/cwfrm.htm

To read about General Silas Casey, Front Royal, Vicksburg in 1863, the Great Snowball battle, and African-American soldiers in the Union army, go to
http://www.thehistorynet.com/THNarchives/CivilWar/

Reconstruction and the Birth of Civil Rights (1865–1877)

To read about the Jim Crow laws, go to
http://www.nps.gov/malu/documents/jim_crow_laws.htm

To see photos of the Jim Crow laws in effect, go to
http://www.ushmm.org/olympics/zcc036a.htm

To learn about Reconstruction, go to
http://www.worldbook.com/fun/aajourny/html/bh054.html

Industrialization (1850–1900)

For photos of immigrants arriving at Ellis Island, go to
http://cmp1.ucr.edu/exhibitions/immigration_id.html

Read about Samuel Slater, the man who built the first mill in America, at
http://www.geocities.com/~woon_heritage/slater.htm

To read about President William McKinley and the Spanish-American War of 1898, go to
http://www.history.ohio-state.edu/projects/McKinley/SpanAmWar.htm

To see photos and read about child labor in 1908, go to
http://www.historyplace.com/unitedstates/childlabor/index.html

To learn about the origins of labor unions, go to
http://www.kentlaw.edu/ilhs/articles.htm

To read about the life and philanthropy of Andrew Carnegie, go to
http://www.pbs.org/wgbh/amex/carnegie/index.html

To learn about inventors and their inventions, head to
http://www.si.edu/resource/faq/nmah/invent.htm

The Twentieth Century
To read about the Mexican Revolution, go to
http://northcoast.com/~spdtom/rev.html

To view photos taken of different parts of the country during the Depression, go to
http://www.corbis.com/experience/FDR/fsa/map.html

Read eyewitness accounts of Lindbergh's flight, the great San Francisco earthquake, President Truman's diary, driving the first automobiles, Teddy Roosevelt's safari to Africa, and child labor at
http://www.ibiscom.com/20frm.htm

To read about women's suffrage and the Nineteenth Amendment, head to
http://www.nara.gov/education/teaching/woman/home.html

Events Since World War II
For information about the Warsaw Pact and NATO, go to
http://encarta.msn.com/find/Concise.asp?ti=047DE000

To read illustrated articles about immigration, Pearl Harbor, Amelia

Earhart, Anne Frank, Rosa Parks, Melba Pettillo, Jackie Robinson, Colin Powell, Sir Edmund Hillary, John Glenn, Neil Armstrong, Buzz Aldrin, and Sally Ride, check out this site. Each story includes time lines and photos.

http://teacher.scholastic.com/century/index.htm

For information and photographs of Martin Luther King Jr., go to

http://users.massed.net/~tstrong/Martin.htm

For photographs of John F. Kennedy, go to

http://www.historyplace.com/kennedy/gallery.htm

To access a history of NASA's *Apollo* program which landed humans on the moon, go to

http://www.hq.nasa.gov/office/pao/History/SP-4214/contents.html

Use the time line at this site to choose articles (with photos) about the civil rights movement from 1954 to 1965, including information on *Brown v. Board of Education*.

http://www.wmich.edu/politics/mlk/

The American Government

To learn about the branches of government, how laws are made, the election process, citizenship, and American symbols, go to

http://bensguide.gpo.gov/

Check out this site to find out how the Air Force was formed and what makes planes fly.

http://www.af.mil/aflinkjr/jr.htm

For information about law enforcement and the Federal Bureau of Investigation (FBI), go to

http://www.fbi.gov/kids/kids.htm

What is government intelligence? How does the CIA use dogs? Which president created the CIA? Find the answers at

http://www.odci.gov/cia/ciakids/

To obtain biographical and contact information about your representatives in Congress as well as information about candidates for office at the national and state levels, go to

http://www.vote-smart.org/

Note: For local government, search using a city or town name and "chamber of commerce."

American Presidents

To access biographies about each of the presidents of the United States, go to

http://gi.grolier.com/presidents/nbk/prescont.html

To find detailed biographies about U.S. presidents, go to

http://www.americanpresidents.org/

Which U.S. presidents were left-handed? Who had the most sisters? To answer those questions and more, go to

http://www.fujisan.demon.co.uk/USPresidents/preslist.htm

To learn about the U.S. presidents and read their inaugural addresses, go to

http://www.historybuff.com/presidents/index.html

To access presidential election results and information about the United States Cabinet, go to

http://www.ipl.org/ref/POTUS/

To visit the presidential libraries of Bush, Carter, Eisenhower, Ford, Hoover, Johnson, Kennedy, Nixon, Reagan, FDR, and Truman, go to

http://www.nara.gov/nara/president/address.html

To read biographies about the first ladies, go to

http://www.whitehouse.gov/WH/glimpse/firstladies/html/firstladies.html

To access a photo and a short biography about each American president, go to

http://www.whitehouse.gov/WH/glimpse/presidents/html/ presidents.html

To read about what it is like to live in the White House, take a virtual tour at

http://www.whitehouse.gov/WH/glimpse/tour/html/index.html

Current Events

At this site you will find a daily list of news stories by categories. Click on the topic and get a set of links to stories posted by various news organizations.

http://www.yahooligans.com/content/news/

This news site lets you choose articles of varying lengths about many different topics, both international and domestic.

http://abcnews.go.com/

Explore stories from two different news magazines at this site. Click on the article titles to get either the whole story or a summary with a link to more information.

http://teacher.scholastic.com/newszone/index.asp

Select national, world, or local news at this site.

http://cbsnews.cbs.com/

This site contains links to international and U.S. newspapers.

http://www.allnewspapers.com/

Read top U.S. and international news stories at this main page or select a subject such as "Space" or "Travel" to explore different stories.

http://www.cnn.com/

To locate local news, go to

http://www.cnn.com/LOCAL/

Go to this site to find and read local newspapers from across the country.

http://www.newspapers.com/

Find news stories on people, animals, weather, and kids' opinion surveys at this site. It also includes an archive of previously published articles.

http://www.pathfinder.com/TFK/

The stories at this site cover the same headline topics as the national broadcast media but includes background information and photos.

http://www.pbs.org/newshour/extra/

3: ENGLISH

GENERAL ENGLISH SOURCES

This guide to grammar and writing has an excellent index that will guide you through everything from adjectives to wordiness. Check your grammar, punctuation, and usage at

http://webster.commnet.edu/HP/pages/darling/grammar.htm

This Internet encyclopedia is a great resource for authors, writing terminology, writing topics, biographies, and report topics. It's located at

http://www.clever.net/com/enc/index.html

Alphabets and Languages

To get definitions or synonyms for English words, as well as information about languages from all over the world, try

http://www.facstaff.bucknell.edu/rbeard/diction.html

This site allows you to enter foreign words and get their English translation, and vice versa! Use the dictionary function to find definitions at

http://www.itools.com/research-it/

To see the sign language equivalent of many English words, go to

http://www.masterstech-home.com/asldict.html

To view the hieroglyphic alphabet, and get English words translated into hieroglyphics, head to

http://www.tourism.egnet.net/cafe/tor_trn.htm

Creative Writing

To find tips for many different kinds of writing, as well as story starters, head to

http://teacher.scholastic.com/writewit/index.htm

For a long list of proverbs, check out

http://www.corsinet.com/braincandy/proverb.html

To learn how to write haiku, go to
http://www.jinjapan.org/kidsweb/index.html

To read work by other students (start with Publisher's Picks) and send in your own for online publication, go to
http://www.kidpub.org/kidpub/

For information about rhyme schemes and how to write poetry, head to
http://www.nesbitt.com/poetry/howto.html

Dictionaries/Encyclopedias

To find out what acronyms, such as NASA, represent and see the world's longest acronym (at the bottom of the page), check out
http://www.acronymfinder.com/about.asp#What

To locate definitions, pronunciations, translations, and rhymes, go to
http://www.itools.com/research-it/

To use a handy thesaurus, make your way to
http://www.thesaurus.com/Roget-Alpha-Index.html

To play a vocabulary building game, as well as definitions and word lists, go to
http://www.vocabulary.com/VUlevelone.html

To use a dictionary, check out
http://www.merriam-webster.com

Letter Sounds and Words

To see a list of palindromes and other interesting word oddities, check out this trivia-packed site at
http://members.aol.com/gulfhigh2/words5.html

To learn about and create anagrams, check out
http://www.anagramfun.com

To find synonyms, homophones, illustrations, and rhyming words, check out
http://www.link.cs.cmu.edu/dougb/rhyme-doc.html

Test yourself on the 50 most commonly misspelled words at
http://www.sentex.net/%7Emmcadams/spelling.html

To search for word origins, go to
http://www.takeourword.com/search.html

To get explanations and see examples of antecedents, clauses, modifiers, and a host of other writing terms, go to
http://www.well.com/~mmcadams/words.html

To explore the origins of words like "Gotham," "blockbuster," and "gizmo," head to
http://www.word-detective.com/backidx.html

Parts of Speech
For practice with plurals, head to
http://www.funbrain.com/plurals/index.html

For practice with is/are and was/were, go to
http://www.funbrain.com/verb/index.html

Check out information and practice tests on punctuation and grammar at
http://www.grammarbook.com/punctuation/fr_punc.html

For explanations of punctuation and pronunciation, go to
http://www.m-w.com/pronguid.htm

Guess the compound word, reorder anagrams, read similes, and practice spelling at
http://www.members.home.net/teachwell/index.htm

To locate rules of pronunciation, quotations, examples of newspaper articles, compound words, spelling, and proper usage, check out the style book at

http://www.theslot.com/contents.html

To avoid making common errors in English, go to

http://www.wsu.edu/~brians/errors/errors.html

Practical Writing

To find biographies of and advice from well-known authors, check out interview transcripts at

http://teacher.scholastic.com/authorsandbooks/authors/library.htm

To find some tips on writing essays, go to

http://thelockbox.tripod.com/essay.html

To locate important and well-known quotes, go to

http://www.bartleby.com/99/

To read some classic poetry, go to

http://www.bartleby.com/verse/

To find biographical information, go to

http://www.biography.com/

To write to your congressional representative, head to

http://www.house.gov/writerep/

A list of postal abbreviations for the United States is located at

http://www.princeton.edu/Main/postal.html

To find a public library near you, practice using the Dewey decimal system, and reserve books, check out

http://www.publiclibraries.com/

Reading Literature

To find lists of Newbery books sorted by category, go to

http://elink.scls.lib.wi.us/mirror/madison/youth/newbcat.html

To find cliches, head to

http://utopia.knoware.nl/users/sybev/cliche/cliche.htm

To read about books that influenced important American figures, check out

http://www.achievement.org/library/frames.html

To access a list of books that won the Newbery Medal, and link to the Caldecott and Coretta Scott King award pages, make your way to

http://www.ala.org/alsc/newbery.html

For a list of the bestselling books in the country, go to

http://www.bookweb.org/booksense/bestsellers/

To read fairy tales, go to

http://www.inform.umd.edu/EdRes/ReadingRoom/Fiction/FairyTales/

Choose one of Aesop's Fables to read (or hear) from a selection of more than 600 at

http://www.pacificnet.net/%7Ejohnr/aesop/

To find myths from around the world, check out this Web site that includes a helpful pronunciation guide.

http://www.pantheon.org/mythica/areas/

To access an electronic index of folklore and mythology, go to

http://www.pitt.edu/~dash/folktexts.html

To have poems read to you or to share your own, go to

http://www.poets.org/

For information about children's authors and illustrators, go to

http://www.scbwi.org/member.htm

Writing Tools

To learn about common idioms, check out
http://www.funbrain.com/idioms/index.html

Learn about plot, point of view, character, setting, and theme by reading a story at
http://www.learner.org/exhibits/literature/

To get examples of similes, go to
http://www.swiftsite.com/ideabank/csmenumain.htm

To make a Venn diagram to analyze or create a story, go to
http://www.venndiagram.com/

For definitions/examples of terms, such as alliteration and cacophony, check the Dictionaries/Encyclopedias section.

4: GEOGRAPHY

◀ GENERAL GEOGRAPHY SOURCES

Need to know your state capitals, birds, and flags? Quiz yourself at
http://edu4kids.com/states

Check out this site to find a huge index of geography-related sites,
with topics such as plate tectonics and erosion at
http://members.aol.com/bowermanb/101.html

At this site you'll receive a brief written description and a photo of a
country you select. In addition, you'll get extensive links to further
your knowledge of that country. Find it at
http://www.3datlas.com/main_co.html

To get statistics on state populations and sizes for the entire United
States, go to
http://www.ipl.org/youth/stateknow/skhome.html

Use this site to find maps, flags, and many other kinds of data for
countries around the world.
http://www.odci.gov/cia/publications/factbook/country.html

Biomes
Find a site with links to photos and text about each of the world's
major biomes at
http://redbaron.bishops.ntc.nf.ca/wells/biomes/index.htm

Definitions and examples of animals found in each type of biome can
be found at
http://ths.sps.lane.edu/biomes/index1.html

For information about plants that grow in different biomes, head to
http://www.kapili.com/plantspot/biomelist.html

Earthquakes

For a list of real-time earthquakes around the world, as well as information about recent and historical earthquakes, go to
http://earthquake.usgs.gov/neis/bulletin/bulletin.html

For links to details about plate tectonics, faults, and major earthquakes, go to the General Earthquake Information page at
http://earthquake.usgs.gov/neis/general/handouts/general_seismicity.html

For an explanation of how earthquakes happen and to see a map of the world's major fault zones, check out this site. It also includes links to historical accounts and photos.
http://www.crustal.ucsb.edu/ics/understanding/

Land, Water, and Air: The Physical World

To find a thorough explanation of the components and structure of the atmosphere, go to
http://encarta.msn.com/find/Concise.asp?ti=02149000

For an explanation of plate tectonics and a diagram showing the movement of the earth's plates, go to
http://observe.ivv.nasa.gov/nasa/earth/tectonics/Tectonics2.html

To check out water data for your local area or any other U.S. region, go to
http://water.usgs.gov/

What is a desert? How many are there in North America? What animals, plants, and people live in them? This site answers these questions and more.
http://www.desertusa.com/life.html

For information about rivers and other bodies of water in the United States, go to the National Park Service site at
http://www.nps.gov/rivers/quotes.html

Information about wild and scenic rivers listed by state is located at
http://www.nps.gov/rivers/wildriverslist.html

To get information about the Galápagos islands and adventures in Antarctica, go to
http://www.terraquest.com/

To view color-coded water supply and precipitation maps of the western U.S., go to
http://www.wcc.nrcs.usda.gov/water/quantity/westwide.html

Maps
To find topographical maps of the world, as well as related resources about flags and population figures, check out
http://plasma.nationalgeographic.com/mapmachine/index.html

To view and download over 230,000 maps of states, countries, and regions sorted by historical, economic, political, population, and other criteria, go to
http://www.lib.utexas.edu/Libs/PCL/Map_collection/
Map_collection.html

This is a collection of more than 800 historical maps spanning nearly 500 years, from the sixteenth century through the early twentieth century. Maps focus on the state of Georgia and surrounding region, but include most of America.
http://www.libs.uga.edu/darchive/hargrett/maps/maps.html

To get street maps of cities in the United States and cities in foreign countries, go to
http://www.mapblast.com/mblast/mAdr.mb

To see a complete map of the sky, as well as images from the Hubble Space Telescope and descriptive text, check out this celestial map at
http://www.nationalgeographic.com/features/97/stars/chart/index.
html

This site allows you to search for a place or named feature, to get state and local street maps, and world thematic maps about birth rate, education levels, and precious metals.
http://www.randmcnally.com/?area=explore_maps&content=explore_maps/explore_maps.ehtml

For clear examples and explanations of what you see on a map, go to http://www.usgs.gov/education/teacher/what-do-maps-show/index.html

People on Land and Water
To see aerial or satellite photos of cities and famous places, go to http://terraserver.microsoft.com/

To learn about the ecosystems of deserts, plains and plateaus, as well as fires, weeds, minerals, and archeology, go to http://www.blm.gov/education/teacher.html

To get current world and United States population data, go to http://www.census.gov/

To get longitude, latitude, and population figures for cities in the United States, check out http://www.census.gov/cgi-bin/gazetteer

To get current U.S. population data about each of the states, go to http://www.census.gov/datamap/www/

For data about foreign countries, including information about economies, defense, geography, government, resources, languages, people, maps, and a whole lot more, go to http://www.emulateme.com

This travel guide includes current weather information and lists of major attractions in countries around the world. Find it at http://www.excite.com/travel/

Volcanoes

To read eyewitness accounts of volcanoes and see some great photos, check out

http://volcano.und.edu/

How hot is a volcano? What good comes from eruptions? These and hundreds more questions are answered here. The site also includes links to live camera views of volcanoes.

http://vulcan.wr.usgs.gov/LivingWith/framework.html

To see a map showing the world's major volcanic regions and to get information about and photos of specific volcanoes, go to

http://www.geo.mtu.edu/volcanoes/world.html

5: MATH

Sites are listed in the General Math Sources section if they apply to more than one math section. In some cases, specific page addresses are also included in the individual sections, such as Graphs or Measurement. Main addresses usually take you to an index page. These sites serve as excellent resources if you have a very broad question or aren't sure where to start.

GENERAL MATH SOURCES

This service provides complete answers to your math questions. Search the site to see if your question has already been answered. If not, send Dr. Math a question by filling out a form on this Web site.

http://forum.swarthmore.edu/dr.math/drmath.elem.html

This site includes games to help you practice math skills. Don't be afraid to challenge yourself with the more difficult levels. Be careful to avoid the ads that look like games.

http://www.funbrain.com/

This site is the place to go to for biographies of mathematicians. Click on a letter of the alphabet or a set of years to get a list of names.

http://www-groups.dcs.st-and.ac.uk/~history/BiogIndex.html

This site provides flash cards, memory games, and matching games to help build speed and accuracy.

http://www.quia.com/math.html

This fun set of interactive games spans grade levels 4 to 10. Each question is created randomly, allowing the opportunity to master any area selected. The choices include basic math functions, bar graphs, map reading, rounding numbers, and many others.

http://www.scienceacademy.com/BI/index.html

You can search the archive at this site to see if the information you need has already been posted in the answer to someone else's question.

http://www.sisweb.com/cgi-bin/swish/mmbfront.pl

This Web site shows problems and their solutions. The solutions are backed up by step-by-step explanations of how the answer was reached.

http://www.webmath.com

Addition, Subtraction, Multiplication, and Division

This site provides information about the four basic math functions in a question and answer format, as well as material about square roots and word problems.

http://forum.swarthmore.edu/dr.math/drmath.elem.html

Practice addition, subtraction, multiplication, and division with simple drills at

http://www.edu4kids.com/math

ArithmAttack is a game that will tell you how many math problems you can solve in 60 seconds. You can even download the game (for free!) and run it on your computer at home. To practice these problems to gain speed, try

http://www.dep.anl.gov/aatack.htm

Practice addition, subtraction, multiplication, and division games at

http://www.funbrain.com/football/index.html

and

http://www.funbrain.com/math/index.html

and

http://www.quia.com/math.html

This site provides 52 levels of addition, subtraction, multiplication, and division problems on worksheets that you can print. Once you have completed them, print out the answer key to check your answers.

http://www.sssoftware.com/freeworksheets/index.html

To get lowest common denominators and fix improper fractions, go to
http://www.webmath.com/fractions.html

For help with word problems, go to
http://www.webmath.com/wordproblems.htm

Computers and Calculators
To read a lengthy article about the history and development of computers, go to

http://www.digitalcentury.com/encyclo/update/comp_hd.html

What exactly is a CPU? To find out, use this dictionary of computing terms at

http://www.instantweb.com/foldoc/index.html

To use a simple calculator, check out

http://www.mathgoodies.com/calculators/calculator.htm

Geometry
Check out the Geometry section of Dr. Math to find the answers to questions about triangles, spheres, polygons, and much more.
http://forum.swarthmore.edu/dr.math/drmath.elem.html

For practice using angles and geometrical terms, choose activities 14 or 16 at

http://www.quia.com/math.html

Graphs
To generate a graph from individual data plots, try this powerful section of WebMath. Be sure to enter your data points with the appropriate parentheses and commas or the site won't understand your request.
http://www.webmath.com/graphing.html

Measurement and Time
For accurate sunrise, sunset, moon phase, and eclipse data, check out

http://aa.usno.navy.mil/AA/data/

Enter a month and year—past or future—into this perpetual calendar and find out the day of the week for historical events or anniversaries.

http://alabanza.com/kabacoff/Inter-Links/cgi/cal.cgi

To see a chart with U.S./metric equivalents as well as a chart demonstrating scientific notation, go to

http://alabanza.com/kabacoff/Inter-Links/misc/weights.html

For information about measurements and conversions, select "Terms and Units of Measure" at

http://forum.swarthmore.edu/dr.math/drmath.elem.html

Need to convert temperatures from Celsius to Fahrenheit? This site will do the trick. Choose the units of temperature you would like to convert from a pull-down menu and then enter the number you want converted. Click "Submit" to get your answer.

http://www.cchem.berkeley.edu/ChemResources/Temperature.html

For practice with area and perimeter problems, try

http://www.funbrain.com/poly/index.html

To find out how different kinds of clocks work, try

http://www.howstuffworks.com/cgi-bin/search.pl

To find out distances between cities around the world, check out

http://www.indo.com/distance/

Do you need to convert centimeters to inches? This conversion calculator will help you get it done. Select the type of conversion you want from the box in the upper left-hand corner of the page. Then press the button that says "Get It!" in the center of the page. A new window containing the conversion will appear. Enter the number you want converted and click "is equal to" for the answer to appear.

http://www.megacalculator.com/_Conv/mc_list.htm

For practice working with measurements and their equivalents, select games 7, 32, or 33 at

http://www.quia.com/math.html

To convert measurement units at this site, note that you have to press the little down arrow to see the list of options. Then, highlight the units you want.

http://www.webmath.com/convert.html

For help calculating the perimeter and area of various shapes, go to

http://www.webmath.com/geo_objects.html

Money and Monetary Systems

For practice making change, try the activity at

http://www.funbrain.com/cashreg/index.html

To discover more about American money and how it is made, as well as to learn about money from other countries, check out

http://www.kidsbank.com

For practice using money, try game 6 at

http://www.quia.com/math.html

To find the proper tip to leave for a meal in a restaurant, go to

http://www.webmath.com/tip.html

Do you wonder how far your allowance would go in Italy? Check out this universal currency converter. It will convert the amount of one currency into the value in the other currency that you select from its list.

http://www.xe.net/ucc/

Numbers and Number Systems

To find questions and answers about Roman numerals, large numbers, place value, and infinity, check out

http://forum.swarthmore.edu/dr.math/drmath.elem.html

To practice your logic skills, check out the games at
http://www.cut-the-knot.com/games.html

For some challenging sequence games, head to
http://www.funbrain.com/cracker/index.html

To practice with fractions, go to
http://www.funbrain.com/fract/index.html

To practice using negative numbers, try the activities at
http://www.funbrain.com/linejump/index.html

For practice using fractions and percents, check out
http://www.quia.com/math.html

To convert decimals and fractions back and forth, go to
http://www.webmath.com/decimals.html

How do you say a very large number? Enter up to 63 digits at
http://www.webmath.com/saynum.html

Statistics and Probability
To see examples of probability problems solved and to browse frequently asked questions about statistics and probability, check out
http://forum.swarthmore.edu/dr.math/tocs/prob.stats.middle.html

To see sample graphs from surveys, go to
http://teacher.scholastic.com/kidusasu/index.htm

For definitions and examples using dice, coins, and playing cards, go to
http://www.homeworkcentral.com/knowledge/vsl_files.htp?fileid=134160&flt=KE

For an explanation of probability that includes example problems, go to
http://www.learner.org/exhibits/dailymath/playing.html

To find the definition of probability and many examples, check out
http://www.mathleague.com/help/percent/percent.htm

6: SCIENCE

GENERAL SCIENCE SOURCES

For general information about space and astronomy, go to
http://kidsastronomy.about.com/kids/kidsastronomy/mbody.htm

Follow the links at this site to articles on photosynthesis, gardening, how to make a pinhole camera, and other subjects.
http://kidscience.about.com/kids/kidscience/mbody.htm

For information about agriculture, go to
http://kidscience.about.com/kids/kidscience/msub18.htm

For information on just about every science topic (from clouds to the International Space Station), check out
http://spacelink.nasa.gov/NASA.Overview/NASA.Fact.Sheets/

Find out how infrared technology works and discover many other explanations of science in the news at
http://whyfiles.news.wisc.edu/welcome/index.html

Consult this ultimate Science Fair Project Resource Guide that includes explanations of the scientific method and links to topic choices, sample projects, and advice.
http://www.ipl.org/youth/projectguide/

For help with science fair projects, go to
http://www.isd77.k12.mn.us/resources/cf/SciProjIntro.html

To find hands-on science activities, complete with directions and diagrams, go to
http://www.mcrel.org/whelmers/
Read the safety rules first!

How can ants survive being in a microwave oven? Why do helium balloons deflate so quickly? Click on these and other nagging questions and find out! The information at this site is well suited for science experiment ideas and reports.

http://www.newscientist.com/lastword/house.html

For information about the science of plants and animals, go to
http://www.newscientist.com/lastword/plants.html

How is science helping to solve modern problems, such as climate warming? Find out at

http://www.ngdc.noaa.gov/ngdc/ngdcsociety.html

Animals

For information on animals ranging from arthropods to zebras, check out this site. You can search for a particular animal or for group names, such as mammals. Each animal listing includes phylum, class, order, and family.

http://animaldiversity.ummz.umich.edu/index.html

For answers to questions about mollusks (shelled animals), go to
http://erato.acnatsci.org/conchnet/facts.html

Check out this site for information about the habitat, diet, and breeding habits of insects. You can see diagrams that identify the parts of common insects.

http://insected.arl.arizona.edu/info.htm

Use this list of links to zoos to search for information on common and uncommon animals not found above.

http://now2000.com/kids/zoos.shtml

To search for information about a particular marine creature, go to
http://seasky.org/search.html

For information about animal gestation periods, go to
http://www.almanac.com/edpicks.0698/gestation.html

Interested in bird watching, bird feeding, bird migration, nest boxes, bird identification, bird habitats, bird profiles, and lovely bird photos? Check out

http://www.birdnature.com/index.html

How fast is a turtle compared to a horse? What do you call a female sheep? Find a list of group, male, female, baby animals' names, plus animal speeds at

http://www.co.fairfax.va.us/library/faq/animal.htm

Need to know about spiders? Go to

http://www.discovery.com/exp/spiders/backyard.html

Check the "What's Hot" section of this site for stories and background facts about pets, wild animals, insects, dinosaur fossils, and more.

http://www.discovery.com/guides/animals/animals.html

For information on birds (the tallest, fastest, and smallest), go to this site.

http://www.enchantedlearning.com/subjects/birds/

For comprehensive information about dinosaurs of all shapes and sizes, go to

http://www.enchantedlearning.com/subjects/dinosaurs/index.html

Do fish sleep? What do lobsters eat? Read the answers to these "fishy" questions at

http://www.nefsc.nmfs.gov/faq/

Did you know that some sponges are big enough for you to fit inside them? Find facts and photos of them plus mollusks, echinoderms, deadly cnidarians (sea stars), and sharks at

http://www.oceanicresearch.org/lesson.html

For photos of oceans, storms, coastal seas, and marine species, browse the collection at

http://www.photolib.noaa.gov

For information and photos about marine invertebrates, go to
http://www.seasky.org/sea2.html

For photos of invertebrates and vertebrates, go to
http://www.si.edu/organiza/museums/zoo/photos/phoset.htm

To find photos and fact sheets about lake, ocean, and river animals, head to
http://www.underwaterworld.com/guide/

Ecology
Check out this site for articles about and photos of natural disasters, deserts, and forests.
http://edcwww.cr.usgs.gov/earthshots/slow/tableofcontents

To learn about how animals and plants use camouflage, head to
http://erato.acnatsci.org/conchnet/facts.html

For links to information about El Niño, hurricanes, the hydrologic cycle, seasons, and tsunamis, go to
http://observe.ivv.nasa.gov/nasa/earth/earth_index.shtml

To learn about the ozone, go to
http://observe.ivv.nasa.gov/nasa/exhibits/ozone/Ozone.html

To find out how much water people use, go to
http://www.almanac.com/edpicks.0698/waterused.html

For information about endangered species and their habitats, go to
http://www.amnh.org/Exhibition/Expedition/Endangered/

Where does your water come from? How is it purified? Use this case study of Philadelphia to investigate your city water supply.
http://www.desertusa.com/life.html

To explore a dictionary of environmental terms, go to
http://www.epa.gov/students/terms_of_environment.htm

To read about the Clean Air Act, sources of pollution, acid rain, and repairing the ozone layer, go to
http://www.epa.gov/students/plain_english_guide_to_the_clean.htm

For information about the monarch butterfly's biology, photos, and conservation go to
http://www.monarchwatch.org/

To monitor monarch butterfly migration, go to
http://www.monarchwatch.org/tagmig/index.htm

To read about amphibians, go to
http://www.mp1-pwrc.usgs.gov/amphib/frogsum.html

To read a discussion of water, wetlands, endangered species, and public lands, go to
http://www.nwf.org/nwf/kids/cool/public1.html

For information about food chains, go to
http://www.planetpals.com/planet.html

To see a slide show about air pollution, go to
http://www-wilson.ucsd.edu/education/airpollution/airpollution.html

Take a virtual walk and learn how common plants and animals connect in the web of life.
http://www.worldbook.com/fun/wbla/camp/html/walk.html

To read about global warming, species extinction, and biological diversity, go to
http://www.worldbook.com/fun/wbla/earth/html/earth.htm

Outer Space
Explore Mars using these images and activities. Learn about superposition, cratering, and slump blocks at
http://cass.jsc.nasa.gov/expmars/activities.html

To get explanations for all sorts of outer space vocabulary, check out
http://ispec.scibernet.com/station/

For an explanation of the Big Bang theory, go to
http://map.gsfc.nasa.gov/html/big_bang.html

At this site you can choose from over 500 NASA images of planets, moons, and asteroids or read fact sheets about the celestial bodies.
http://nssdc.gsfc.nasa.gov/imgcat/

For information on how a star is created, go to
http://observe.ivv.nasa.gov/nasa/exhibits/stellarbirth/Star_index.html

For information on star evolution and death, go to
http://observe.ivv.nasa.gov/nasa/space/stellardeath/
stellardeath_intro.html

To see pictures taken by the Hubble Space Telescope, including images of star clusters, galaxies, and quasars, and read about the expanding universe, go to
http://oposite.stsci.edu/pubinfo/pictures.html

To go on a tour of the solar system and get photos, facts, and information, head to
http://seasky.org/sky7.html

Is the sun shrinking? What is a flare? When is the earth closest to the sun? Find these answers under the "Ask a Solar Physicist" link. For information about the sun, go to
http://solar-center.stanford.edu/

To learn about constellations and see photos of galaxies and nebula, go to
http://www.astro.wisc.edu/~dolan/constellations/

For information about black holes and neutron stars, go to
http://www.eclipse.net/~cmmiller/BH/blkmain.html

Go here for statistics, facts, names, biographies, spacecraft and rocket details, information on foreign space programs, and history data.

http://www.friends-partners.org/~mwade/spaceflt.htm

To learn the constellations, play this game that will give you clues to their names and then show you what they look like in the sky.

http://www.funbrain.com/constellation/index.html

To read an illustrated article about galaxy types, clusters, and the history of their discovery, go to

http://www.icu2.net/faahomepage/galaxies.htm

If you need information about past space exploration, go to

http://www.ksc.nasa.gov/history/history.html

For breaking news and coverage of missions to outer space, go to the NASA home page at

http://www.nasa.gov/

To find comparison data about the planets in this solar system, as well as comet data, check out

http://www.nasm.edu/ceps/ETP/

Choose from more than 950 images of the sun, planets, asteroids, comets, NASA spacecraft, and historical programs at

http://www.solarviews.com/eng/homepage.htm

For information about the nine planets in our solar system, go to

http://www.tcsn.net/afiner/

The Physical World

See momentum and centripetal force in action at

http://observe.ivv.nasa.gov/nasa/exhibits/toys_space/toyframe.html

To read about and see demonstrations involving physics topics such as light, atoms, waves, gravity, magnetism, electricity, relativity, and

much more, go to

http://www.brainpop.com/indexwin.asp

For explanations of elements, states of matter, chemical reactions, and atoms, go to

http://www.chem4kids.com/

Why is grass green? What four colors do printers use? Check out this site about color in science and art.

http://www.cs.iupui.edu/~pellison/colorworm/home.html

Check out animated demonstrations of electricity, waves, and more at this site. In particular, check out the animated pendulum. Change its mass, gravity level, and string length and see what happens.

http://www.energy.ca.gov/education/index.html

To view a periodic table and see atomic maps showing electron shells, go to

http://www.eudoxos.de/java/periodic/index.html

To find out about the history of wheels and gears, as well as to find useful examples of simple machines and overcoming inertia and friction, go to

http://www.exploratorium.edu/cycling/

For an explanation of light, check out

http://www.fnal.gov/pub/light/

To see how roller coasters make use of physics (acceleration, energy, and friction), go to

http://www.learner.org/exhibits/parkphysics/

To find activities about energy, light, electricity, and atoms, go to

http://www.miamisci.org/af/sln/

Need to know about electrons? Go to

http://www.nmsi.ac.uk/online/electron/

To learn about waves (including sound, light, and X rays) go to
http://www.smgaels.org/physics/home.htm

Planet Earth
To learn about how fossils form and about different rock types, go to
http://encarta.msn.com/find/Concise.asp?z=1&pg=2&ti=031C3000

To ask questions of a professional geologist, go to
http://walrus.wr.usgs.gov/docs/ask-a-ge.html/

To see photos and samples of fossils plus information on how to collect and care for them, go to
http://web.ukonline.co.uk/conker/fossils/index.htm

To find the places with the highest elevations in the United States, go to
http://www.americasroof.com/usa.shtml

To find the locations with the highest elevations in the world, go to
http://www.americasroof.com/world.html

To read about the earth's formation and listen to geologists discuss various topics, go to
http://www.discovery.com/guides/earth/earth.html

To learn about the physical features of the world's oceans, and get historical information and water cycle data, go to
http://www.mos.org/oceans/planet/index.html

To find out what minerals are mined in your state and what they are used for, go to
http://www.msha.gov/KIDS/MINING.HTM

For information about the atmosphere, go to
http://www.pbs.org/wgbh/nova/balloon/science/atmosphere.html

To learn about continental drift, go to
http://www.tyrrellmuseum.com/tour/contdrft.html

For information about sedimentary rock, go to
http://www.tyrrellmuseum.com/tour/sedirock.html

To see a geologic time line, go to
http://www.tyrrellmuseum.com/tour/timescal.html

For information on the history of geology, go to
http://www.ucmp.berkeley.edu/exhibit/geology.html

For information and photos of 15 common minerals, check out this site. Don't miss the links at the bottom to pages explaining igneous, sedimentary, and metamorphic rocks.
http://www.willowgrove.district96.k12.il.us/RocksandMinerals/4thGradeRocks.html

Plants
Check out these fact sheets for information about many kinds of plants.
http://plant-materials.nrcs.usda.gov:90/pmc/factsheets.html

How do plants defend themselves? Find out about tree shapes, chemicals, and seeds at
http://www.muohio.edu/dragonfly/trees.htmlx

To find out how trees benefit society and the environment, go to
http://www.tesser.com/plantit/benefits.htm

Scientists/Inventors
Who invented the Slinky? What did Edison invent? Use this alphabetical list to find inventions or to search for information on a specific inventor.
http://web.mit.edu/afs/athena.mit.edu/org/i/invent/www/archive.html

To read interviews with current scientists who are changing the way we live, go to
http://www.sciam.com/interview/index.html

Weather

To see temperature, wind chill, and humidity maps, go to
http://groundhog.sprl.umich.edu/index.html

To learn about wind chill and use a wind-chill calculator, go to
http://observe.ivv.nasa.gov/nasa/earth/wind_chill/chill_home.html

To read weather predictions, go to
http://www.almanac.com/siteindex.html

For news of current storms and background stories about extreme weather such as avalanches, tornadoes, and hurricanes, go to
http://www.discovery.com/guides/weather/weather.html

To get information from the United States National Weather Service, go to
http://www.nws.noaa.gov/regions.shtml

To get your local current weather forecast, go to
http://www.weather.com/

To see what weather conditions are like around the world, go to
http://www.wmo.ch/Web-en/member_g.html

What's Life All About?

For images and data about protists, go to
http://megasun.bch.umontreal.ca/protists/gallery.html

For fun facts and photos about fungi, check out
http://www.herb.lsa.umich.edu/kidpage/factindx1.htm

Check out this collection of short articles about curious, newsworthy, dangerous, heroic, ancient, and strange microbes in our environment.
http://commtechlab.msu.edu/sites/dlc-me/

7: WORLD HISTORY

GENERAL HISTORY SOURCES

To read about the Seven Wonders of the Ancient World, go to

http://ce.eng.usf.edu/pharos/wonders/

To learn more about historical topics, conduct a search at

http://encarta.msn.com/

Search for information and find out what happened "On This Day in History" at

http://www.historychannel.com

Ancient Egypt

For information about the Sumerians, Babylonians, Assyrians, and Persians, check out

http://emuseum.mankato.msus.edu/history/middle_east/index.shtml

To read about the daily life, art, hieroglyphics, maps, architecture, and religion of ancient Egypt, go to

http://emuseum.mankato.msus.edu/prehistory/egypt/index.shtml

To explore information about the pyramids of Giza, check out this site. Be sure to explore the data-packed links.

http://library.thinkquest.org/15924/

Who were the Nubians? To find out, check the maps, photos, and text at this site.

http://library.thinkquest.org/22845/

For information about daily life in ancient Egypt, go to

http://members.aol.com/Donnclass/Egyptlife.html

To learn about ancient Egypt, pyramids, mummies, and Cleopatra, go to

http://www.discovery.com/guides/history/egypt.html

To read about the Egyptian Necropolis, the Valley of Kings, or the tomb of the sons of King Ramses, or to go behind the scenes of an archeological dig, head to

http://www.kv5.com/intro.html

Who built the pyramids? How old are they? Find the answers at

http://www.pbs.org/wgbh/nova/pyramid/explore/

Did you know there were black Pharaohs? Read about Nubian culture at

http://www.pbs.org/wonders/fr_e1.htm

Stone Age
To find out how people lived in the Stone Age, click on "Meet the Shaman" at

http://museums.ncl.ac.uk/archive/menu.html

Ancient Greece and Rome
For information about ancient Athens, Amazons, Ionians, Phoenicians, Dorians, Myceneans, Minoans, Homer, and the *Odyssey*, go to

http://emuseum.mankato.msus.edu/prehistory/aegean/index.shtml

To read about daily life in ancient Greece, including information on pets, toys, food, and clothing, go to

http://members.aol.com/Donnclass/Greeklife.html

For information about daily life in ancient Rome, go to

http://members.aol.com/Donnclass/Romelife.html

Ancient European History
Learn about the Etruscans (ancient people of Italy) at

http://www.agmen.com/etruscans/pag_engl/index.htm

Ancient Asia
For information about ancient Chinese culture, go to

http://emuseum.mankato.msus.edu/prehistory/china/index.shtml

To explore China's great cities, or learn about Chinese art and medicines, the Chinese Cultural Revolution, and relations with Hong Kong and Tibet, go to

http://library.thinkquest.org/26469/index2.html

For information about daily life in ancient China, go to
http://members.aol.com/Donnclass/Chinalife.html

To read about daily life in ancient India, go to
http://members.aol.com/Donnclass/Indialife.html

To see a time line of Chinese history that includes links to photos, maps, and information about Chinese dynasties and government, go to
http://www-chaos.umd.edu/history/time_line.html

To learn about the Indus Valley (ancient India/Pakistan), go to
http://www.harappa.com/har/har0.html

To read about the ancient Harappa culture of India, including some of the world's earliest writing, go to

http://www.harappa.com/welcome.html

For information about ancient Japan, check out the history section of this site.

http://www.jinjapan.org/kidsweb/index.html

Learn about modern Indian clothing, festivals, arts, languages, imports/exports, and religions at

http://www.welcometoindia.com/home.html

The Byzantine and Muslim Empires (527–1917)
To read about key figures, costumes, and food in Rome during the Byzantine Era, go to

http://jeru.huji.ac.il/ed1.htm

To read about key figures, costumes, and food in the early Muslim Age, go to
http://jeru.huji.ac.il/ee1.htm

To read about key figures, costumes, and food in the Ottoman period, go to

http://jeru.huji.ac.il/eh1.htm

To read about the Byzantine war on Rome, go to
http://www.thehistorynet.com/MilitaryHistory/articles/1999/
1099_cover.htm

African History
To read about several African cultures, including the Ashanti, Maasai, and Kung San, go to

http://emuseum.mankato.msus.edu/cultural/oldworld/africa.html

To read about the European colonization of Africa, go to
http://kanga.pvhs.chico.k12.ca.us/~bsilva/projects/scramble/index.
html

Ancient American History
To check out an Aztec calendar, Mayan glyphs, and a Mayan civilization time line, go to

http://ancienthistory.about.com/education/ancienthistory/msub8.htm

To read about and see photos of the native peoples of North and South America, check out

http://emuseum.mankato.msus.edu/cultural/newworld/index.shtml

European History
To view the text of the Magna Carta, head to

http://eawc.evansville.edu/anthology/magnacarta.htm

To read about the key figures, costumes, food, and places of the Crusades, go to

http://jeru.huji.ac.il/ef1.htm

To read about the Hundred Years' War and find links to details on major battles, people, and terms, go to

http://looksmart.infoplease.com/ce5/CE024810.html

To read biographies of world explorers, check out
http://www.bham.wednet.edu/explore.htm

For information about the French Revolution and Napoleon, go to
http://www.france.com/culture/history/revolution.html

Why did medieval homes have such tiny windows? How did trade lead to the fall of feudalism? Use this site to learn about homes, health, towns, clothing, and religion in the Middle Ages.
http://www.learner.org/exhibits/middleages/feudal.html

To learn about the Renaissance, go to
http://www.learner.org/exhibits/renaissance/index.html

To learn about Sir Francis Drake and his voyage around the world, go to
http://www.mcn.org/2/oseeler/drake.htm

The Modern World (1700–Present)
For information about the United States in the modern world, see the chapter on American History.

For information about the League of Nations, go to
http://encarta.msn.com/find/Concise.asp?z=1&pg=2&ti=021C8000

Read articles concerning the history, government, religion, and society of many countries.
http://lcweb2.loc.gov/frd/cs/cshome.html

To read illustrated articles about the Battle of Normandy, head to
http://normandy.eb.com/

To see photographs of World War II in the Pacific, check out this site. A link at the bottom of the page will take you to a time line.
http://www.historyplace.com/unitedstates/pacificwar/index.html

To view a time line of the Holocaust that includes descriptions of major events and links to numerous photos, go to
http://www.historyplace.com/worldwar2/holocaust/timeline.html

To view a time line of World War II in Europe, go to this site. To view photographs on the same subject, use the link at the bottom of the page.
http://www.historyplace.com/worldwar2/timeline/ww2time.htm

To read primary documents, eyewitness accounts, and images of World War I, go to
http://www.lib.byu.edu/~rdh/wwi/

Check out the history and purpose of the United Nations at
http://www.un.org/aboutun/

To learn about the events and people involved in the Holocaust, go to
http://www.ushmm.org/outreach/

8: GENERAL HOMEWORK HELP

Most "Homework Help" sites are sets of links to search engines or lists of sites that other people have collected using search engines. While you can get lucky and go right to a set of links that will help you, more likely you will spend hours surfing the sites instead of collecting the information you need to do your homework. However, if you have already checked the specific and general sources listed in the preceding chapters and have not found what you need, here are a few "Homework Help" resources to try:

The subjects on the upper left-hand portion of this page are very helpful. In particular, click on "Science/Nature" and "Space & Astronomy" for useful information.

http://www.about.com/kids

To ask a librarian a question and receive a list of links to helpful resources by e-mail within two days, go to

http://www.ala.org/ICONN/AskKC.html

To access a set of links organized by subject, check out this site. Be sure to check the special topics at the bottom of the page.

http://www.ipl.org/youth/

For a set of links containing information on a wide variety of homework subjects, check out

http://homeworkhelp.about.com

and

http://www.ala.org/parentspage/greatsites/amazing.html

and

http://www.bjpinchbeck.com/

and

http://www.geocities.com/jk_102/

To access articles about a variety of subjects, go to
http://lycoszone.lycos.com/homework.html

At this site you can find an expert who will answer your question via e-mail. All you have to do is pick the subject in which you need assistance.

http://www.askanexpert.com/

9: INDEX